SUSAN WILL M[...] INSPIRE Y[...], FILL YOUR HEART WITH JOY!

"Susan Polis Schutz remains one of the most popular poets in America today, and her work touches virtually everyone."
—Associated Press

"Susan Polis Schutz's popularity can be attributed to her ability to verbalize intimate, honest emotions, shared, but unsaid by most people. Her ability to write simply and honestly of the deepest emotions strikes a responsive chord with readers. . . .Stephen beautifully illustrates Susan's poems. They are a team and their books reflect this."
—Woman's Day

"The appeal of Susan Polis Schutz's poetry and Stephen Schutz's sensitive illustrations is not just that we, as women, as mothers, as members of 'her' generation, can identify. . .she shares with us the most poignant moments of caring for her children."
—Baby Talk

"One picks up Susan's poetry and reads it to the quiet and tasteful accompaniment of Stephen's art and suddenly you are with friends you want to know, and to speak with more."
—Saturday Evening Post

Other books by

Susan Polis Schutz

Come Into the Mountains, Dear Friend
I Want to Laugh, I Want to Cry
Peace Flows from the Sky
Someone Else to Love
Yours If You Ask
Love, Live & Share
Find Happiness in Everything You Do
Don't Be Afraid to Love

Take Charge of Your Body
by Susan Polis Schutz and Katherine F. Carson, M.D.

CONTENTS

This book is dedicated and written with a lot of love to my beautiful daughter, Jordanna Polis Schutz.

I also want to express my deepest love to my two wonderful sons, Jared and Jorian, and of course to my perfect partner in life and love, Stephen. And since I am a daughter, as well as a mother, this book is special for my own loving mother.

INTRODUCTION

When I gave birth to my daughter, I never knew what a very
special relationship a mother and daughter could have. As my
daughter got older and started to understand more about being a
female, I felt as if I were going through all the stages of growing
up once again. I felt a very strong urge to protect her from
anything that could possibly hurt her, but I knew that if I did
this, it would hurt her later on because she would not be
prepared to face the real world. So instead, I tried to show her
and explain to her what I consider to be the important things
in life.

Our mother-daughter relationship is comprised of a very deep
understanding of and support for each other, and it is based on
an enormous amount of emotion and love. There is no other
relationship in the world where two women are so much
like one.

> My beautiful daughter,
>   if I have provided you with an insight
>   into most of the important things in life
>   then I have succeeded
>   as a mother
>   in what I hoped to accomplish in raising you
>   If many of these things slipped by
>   while we were all so busy
>   I have a feeling that you know them anyway
>   One thing I am sure of, though
>   I have taught you to be proud of the fact
>   that you are a woman equal to all men and
>   I have taught you the importance of the family
>   I have loved you every second of your life
>   I have supported you at all times
>   and as a mother, as a person, and as a friend
>   I will always continue to cherish and love
>   everything about you
>   my beautiful daughter

Susan Polis Schutz

To My Daughter

My day always becomes wonderful
when I see your
pretty face smiling so sweetly
There is such warmth and intelligence
radiating from you
It seems that every day
you grow smarter and more beautiful
and every day
I am more proud to be your mother
As you go through all the many stages of life
you should be aware that there will be many times
when you will feel scared and confused
but with your strength and values
you will always end up wiser
and you will have grown from your experiences
understanding more about people and life
I have already gone through
all these stages
So if you need advice or someone to talk to
to make sense out of it all
I hope that you will talk to me
as I am continually rooting for your happiness
my sweet daughter
and I love you

To My Daughter, with Love,
on the Important Things in Life

A mother tries to provide her daughter
with insight into the important things in life
in order to make her life
as happy and fulfilling as possible

A mother tries to teach her daughter
to be good, always helpful to other people
to be fair, always treating others equally
to have a positive attitude at all times
to always make things right when they are wrong
to know herself very well
to know what her talents are
to set goals for herself
to not be afraid of working too hard to reach her goals...

(continued)

...A mother tries to teach her daughter
to have many interests to pursue
to laugh and have fun every day
to appreciate the beauty of nature
to enter into friendships with good people
to honor their friendships and always be a true friend
to appreciate the importance of the family
and to particularly respect and love our elder members
to use her intelligence at all times
to listen to her emotions
to adhere to her values

A mother tries to teach her daughter
to not be afraid to stick to her beliefs
to not follow the majority when the majority is wrong
to carefully plan a life for herself
to vigorously follow her chosen path
to enter into a relationship with someone worthy of herself
to love this person unconditionally with her body and mind
to share all that she has learned in life with this person...

If I have provided you with an insight
into most of these things
then I have succeeded
as a mother
in what I hoped to accomplish in raising you
If many of these things slipped by
while we were all so busy
I have a feeling that you know them anyway
One thing I am sure of, though
I have taught you to be proud of the fact
that you are a woman equal to all men and
I have loved you every second of your life
I have supported you at all times
and as a mother, as a person, and as a friend
I will always continue to cherish and love
everything about you
my beautiful daughter

I love you every minute of every day,
my beautiful daughter

I looked at you today
and saw the same beautiful eyes
that looked at me with love
when you were a baby
I looked at you today
and saw the same beautiful mouth
that made me cry when you first smiled at me
when you were a baby
It was not long ago
that I held you in my arms
long after you fell asleep
and I just kept rocking you
all night long
I looked at you today
and saw my beautiful daughter
no longer a baby
but a beautiful person
with a full range of emotions and feelings
and ideas and goals
Every day is exciting
as I continue to watch you grow
And I want you to always know that
in good and in bad times
I will love you
and that no matter what you do
or how you think
or what you say
you can depend on
my support, guidance
friendship and love
every minute of every day
I love being your mother

I love you so much, my beautiful daughter
I wish that you could see yourself
as others see you—
a sensitive, pretty, loving, intelligent person
who has all the qualities necessary to
become a very successful and beautiful woman
yet sometimes you seem to
have a low opinion of yourself
You compare yourself unfavorably
to others
I wish that you would only judge yourself
according to your own standards
and not be so hard on yourself
I look forward to the day when
you look in the mirror
and for the first time in your life
you see the extraordinary person
that you really are
and you realize how much
you are loved and appreciated
I love you so much
my beautiful daughter
forever as your mother
and friend

I hope that you
will have as much
confidence in yourself
as we have for you.

Some people will be your friend
because of whom you know
Some people will be your friend
because of your position
Some people will be your friend
because of the way you look
Some people will be your friend
because of your possessions
But the only real friends
are the people who will be your friends
because they like you for how you are inside

Try to choose your friends carefully. Make sure that they are worthy of you.

*know that lately you
have been having problems
and I just want you to know
that you can rely on me
for anything
you might need
But more important
keep in mind at all times
that you are very capable
of dealing with any complications
that life has to offer
So
do whatever you must
feel whatever you must
and keep in mind at all times
that we all
grow wiser and
become more sensitive and
are able to enjoy life more
after we go through
hard times*

y dear daughter
you have come out of a time
mingled with problems
wiser, happier
and so much smarter
I am so proud of the way
you handled yourself
the way you thought out the proper solutions
and the strength you used in following through
I no longer have to worry about you
You are very capable of leading your own life
and I know any decisions
that you make for yourself
will be right
You can't imagine how happy this makes me
You are a wonderful person and
a beautiful daughter
I love you dearly, as your mother
and I also love you, as your friend

*ove is
being happy for the other person
when they are happy
being sad for the person
when they are sad
being together in good times
and being together in bad times
Love is the source of strength*

*Love is
being honest with yourself at all times
being honest with the other person at all times
telling, listening, respecting the truth
and never pretending
Love is the source of reality*

*Love is
an understanding that is so complete that
you feel as if you are a part
of the other person
accepting the other person
just the way they are
and not trying to change them
to be something else
Love is the source of unity*

*Love is
the freedom to pursue your own desires
while sharing your experiences
with the other person
the growth of one individual alongside of
and together with the growth
of another individual
Love is the source of success*

Love is
    the excitement of planning things together
    the excitement of doing things together
Love is the source of the future

Love is
    the fury of the storm
    the calm in the rainbow
Love is the source of passion

Love is
    giving and taking in a daily situation
    being patient with each other's
      needs and desires
Love is the source of sharing

Love is
    knowing that the other person
    will always be with you
      regardless of what happens
    missing the other person when they are away
    but remaining near in heart at all times
Love is the source of security

Love is
    the
source
  of
life

Love is the most important emotion that you will ever have. I hope that you are able to open yourself up to a beautiful love. I have tried to express what love means to me. You will discover your own meaning.

Finding the right person to love
is so important
Love comes naturally
but you must both work
at making it last
and try your hardest
at all times
to be fair and honest with each other

Strive for your own goals
and help your mate achieve his
Always try to understand him
Always let him know what you are thinking
Always try to support him
Try to successfully blend
your lives together
with enough freedom
to grow as individuals
Always consider each day you spend together
as a special day
Regardless of what events
occur in your lives
make sure that your
relationship always flourishes
and that you always
love and respect each other

Don't be afraid
to love someone
totally and completely
Love is the most fulfilling
and beautiful feeling in the world
Don't be afraid that you will
get hurt
or that the other person
won't love you as much
There is a risk in
everything you do
and the rewards
are never so great
as what love can bring
So let yourself get involved
completely and honestly
and enjoy the possibility
that what happens
might be the only real
source of happiness

My darling daughter
I am so glad that
you were born in an age
when women are so
aware of what is going on
and don't always have
to fight so hard to be heard
The world is wide open
for you to be whatever you want
It will be hard
but at least you
will find other women
striving for the same thing
and you won't be called "crazy"
for wanting to achieve your goals
Though full equality
is a long way off
there certainly have been changes
that will make your life as a woman
not so stereotyped and confined
You are living in an age
where womanhood is
    finally growing
to be everything
that it can be
My darling daughter
I have watched you play with
    dolls and trucks
footballs and toads
and I see you
    my beautiful child
as a beautiful woman
in full control of her life

*It is very difficult
for a woman
to have a
successful career and
happy children and an
exciting personal life*

When attending to work
most women feel guilty
because they are not with their children
When attending to their children
most women feel guilty
because they have work to do
And if there is time
for personal things
most women feel guilty
because they are neither
attending to the needs of their children
nor their work

In order for a woman
to successfully do
all the things she wants to
she must delegate the things
she does not want to do—
and her husband must equally
share all the family responsibilities
Otherwise
all the demands on the woman
leave her too tired and frustrated
to enjoy life
And that just isn't fair

any women
I have talked to lately
tell me that they are
extremely unfulfilled
being housewives
that their work all day
is so unimportant
that they are not using
their minds—
These women must
do something that
interests them
but they must also
be reassured that
being a good mother is a
very important job
and that just because society
seems to say that raising children
is a menial task
there is no reason to believe this
In fact many beliefs that society
imposes on the individual
are wrong
Women must realize
that whatever they do
is important
as long as they do it well

A woman will get only what she seeks
You must choose your goals carefully
Know what you like
and what you do not like
Be critical about what you can do well
and what you cannot do well
Choose a career or lifestyle that interests you
and work hard to make it a success
Enter a relationship that is worthy of
everything you are physically and mentally capable of
Be honest with people, help them if you can
but don't depend on anyone to make life easy
or happy for you
Only you can do that for yourself
Strive to achieve all that you like
Find happiness in everything you do
Love with your entire being
Love with an uninhibited soul
Make a triumph
of every aspect
of your life

You deserve a life of happiness.

*We cannot
listen to what
others want us
to do
We must listen
to ourselves
We don't need to
copy other people's ways
and we don't need to
act out certain lifestyles
to impress other people
Only we know
and only we can do what
is right for us
So start right now
You will need to
work very hard
You will need to
overcome many obstacles
You will need to go
against the better
judgment of many people
and you will need to
bypass their prejudices
But you can have
whatever you want
if you try hard enough
So start right now and
you will live
a life designed
by you and for you
and you will
love your life*

*Only you
can choose the
lifestyle you
want to
follow.*
SPS

Live Your World of Dreams

*L*ean against a tree
and dream your world of dreams
Work hard at what you like to do
and try to overcome all obstacles
Laugh at your mistakes
and praise yourself for learning from them
Pick some flowers
and appreciate the beauty of nature
Say hello to strangers
and enjoy the people you know
Don't be afraid to show your emotions
laughing and crying make you feel better
Love your friends and family with your entire being
They are the most important part of your life
Feel the calmness on a quiet sunny day
and plan what you want to accomplish in life
Find a rainbow
and live your
world of dreams

*Always have dreams.
Always try to make
them a reality.*

You Are One of Those Rare People
Whose Dreams Will Become a Reality

What makes people succeed
is the fact that they have confidence in themselves
and a very strong sense of purpose
They never have excuses for not doing something
and always try their hardest for perfection
They never consider the idea of failing
and they work extremely hard towards their goals
They know who they are
and they understand their weaknesses
as well as their strong points
They can accept and benefit from criticism
and they know when to defend what they are doing
They are creative people
who are not afraid to be a little different
You are one of these rare people
and it is so exciting to watch you
on your path to success
as you follow your dreams
and make them a reality

I Am Always Here for You

I suspect that
you are thinking about something
that is bothering you
Please share any problems
that you might be having
with someone (it doesn't matter with whom)
because if you just keep these problems in your mind
you will not be able to pursue
your thoughts and activities
to your fullest potential
nor will you be able to enjoy
all the great things in life
because problems, whether they are large or small
often dominate one's thoughts
You are such a wonderful person
and you should always be happy
and free from nagging worries

I want to remind you that
I am always ready to
listen and understand you
and if you ever need me
I am always here for you

ometimes I talk to you
and I am not really sure
what you are thinking
It is so important
to let your feelings
be known
Talk to someone
Write your feelings down
Create something based on your feelings
but do not keep them inside
Never be afraid to
be honest with people
and certainly never be afraid to
be honest with yourself
You are such an
interesting, sensitive, intelligent person
who has so much to share
I want you to know
that wherever you go
or whatever you do
or whatever you think
you can always depend
on me, your mother
for complete and absolute
understanding
support
and love
forever

lder people
could teach us
so much
if we would
only listen
Their wisdom
their simplicity
their experiences
their many years of living
We need them to
live with us
with our families
to teach us
and our children
all they know
to love us
and to let us
love them
and to let us
help them
when they
need it
A family
is not complete
without its
eldest
members

he love
of a family
is so
uplifting

The warmth
of a family
is so
comforting

The support
of a family
is so reassuring

The attitude
of a family
towards
each other
molds one's
attitude forever
towards the
world

I Want You to Live a Life of Love, My Daughter

We brought you into this world
a beautiful little girl
born of love
who would one day
grow up to be
a beautiful woman full of love

I tried to teach you
all the important values
I tried to show you
how to be strong and honest, gentle and sensitive
I tried to explain to you
the importance of achieving your own goals
I tried to express
the need to reach out to people
I tried to emphasize
the beauty of nature
I tried to demonstrate
the extreme importance of the family
And I tried, every day, to set an example
that you could look up to

When we brought you into the world
I did not think about how everything
could be destroyed in a few minutes
in our world not at peace
in our world with nuclear weapons

I taught you love
in a hateful world
because it is love that can abolish hate
before hate abolishes us

I am very sorry, my beautiful daughter
that these destructive forces
have been handed down to you
All of the mothers
and all of the fathers
in the entire world
must unite together and
dedicate ourselves to
ending violence as a way of solving
international problems
We must do this so that we can assure you
my daughter, and all children
that you will grow up
to hike in the mountains
and run in the fields of flowers
so that we can assure you
that you will have a chance to grow up
to live a life
of peace and
love

You are a shining
example of what a
daughter can be —
love and laughter
beautiful and good
honest and principled
determined and independent
sensitive and intelligent
You are a shining
example of what every
mother wishes her
daughter was
and I
am so very
proud of
you

f you know yourself well
and have developed a sense
of confidence in yourself
If you are honest with yourself
and honest with others
If you follow your heart
and adhere to your own truths
you are ready to share yourself
you are ready to set goals
you are ready to find happiness
And the more you love
and the more you give
and the more you feel
the more you will receive
from love
and the more you will receive
from life

The freer you are with your emotions and feelings, the more you will be able to give and receive love.

S ometimes you
think that you
need to be perfect
that you cannot
make mistakes
At these times
you put so much
pressure on yourself
I wish that you
would realize
that you are
a human being—
like everyone else
capable of
reaching great potential
but not capable of
being perfect
So please
just do your best
and realize that
this is enough
Don't compare yourself
to anyone
Be happy to be
the wonderful
unique, very special
person that you are

friend is
someone who is concerned
with everything you do

A friend is
someone who is concerned
with everything you think

A friend is
someone to call upon
during good times

A friend is
someone to call upon
during bad times

A friend is
someone who understands
whatever you do

A friend is
someone who tells you the truth
about yourself

A friend is
someone who knows
what you are going through at all times

A friend is
someone who refuses to listen
to gossip about you

A friend is
someone who supports you
at all times

A friend is
someone who does not
compete with you

A friend is
someone who is genuinely happy for you
when things go well

A friend is
someone who tries to cheer you up
when things don't go well

A friend is
an extension of yourself
without which
you are not complete

Everyone needs people to
understand them throughout
life. I hope that you have at least
one good friend for life. I
have tried to define what a
friend is to me...

My Daughter

Since you were born
you have been
such a beautiful
addition to our family
Now that you are growing up
I can see that
you are a beautiful
addition to the world
and I am so
proud of you
As we watch you
doing things on your own
we know you will find
happiness and success
because we are confident in
your ability
your self-knowledge
your values
But if you ever need a boost
or just someone to talk to
about difficulties
that might be occurring
we are always here
to help you
to understand you
to support you
and to love
you

I Love Your Beautiful Smile, My Daughter

Sometimes I see you
confused
Sometimes I see you
troubled
Sometimes I see you
hurt
and I feel so sad and
helpless
I wish that I could absorb
these feelings from you
and make everything better
but I know that these feelings
will only help you to grow
and understand more about life
These feelings will help you
to become a more sensitive person
So as I watch your eyes
which tell me everything
I will offer you my
understanding and support
I will offer you my
tears and love
I will offer you the
promise that your beautiful
smile will soon return

My daughter
when you were born
I held you in my arms
and just kept smiling at you
You always smiled back
your big eyes wide open
full of love
You were such a
beautiful
good
sweet baby
Now
as I watch you grow up
and become your own person
I look at you
your laughter
your happiness
your simplicity
your beauty
and I wonder where you will be
in fifteen years
and I wonder
where the world will be
in fifteen years
I just hope that you will
be able to enjoy a life
of sensitivity
goodness
accomplishment
and love
in a world that is at peace
But most of all
I want you to know that
I am very proud of you
and that I love you dearly

To My Wonderful Daughter

To see you happy —
laughing and dancing
smiling and content
striving towards goals of your own
accomplishing what you set out to do
having fun with yourself and your friends
capable of loving and being loved
is what I always wished for you

Today I thought about your beautiful face
and felt your excitement for life
and your genuine happiness
and I, as your mother, burst with pride
as I realized that my dreams for you came true
What an extraordinary person you have become
and as you continue to grow
please remember always
how very much
I love you

ABOUT THE AUTHORS

Susan began her writing career at the age of seven, producing a neighborhood newspaper for her friends in the small country town of Peekskill, New York, where she was raised. Upon entering her teen years, she began writing poetry as a means of understanding her feelings. For Susan, writing down what she was thinking and feeling brought clarity and understanding to her life, and today she heartily recommends this to everyone. She continued her writing as she attended and graduated from Rider College, where she majored in English and biology. She then entered a graduate program in physiology, while at the same time teaching elementary school in Harlem and contributing freelance articles to newspapers and magazines.

Stephen Schutz, a native New Yorker, spent his early years studying drawing and lettering as a student at the High School of Music and Art in New York City. He went on to attend M.I.T., where he received his undergraduate degree in physics. During this time, he continued to pursue his great interest in art by taking classes at the Boston Museum of Fine Art. He later entered Princeton University, where he earned his doctoral degree in theoretical physics.

It was in 1965, at a social event at Princeton, that Susan and Stephen met, and their love affair began. Together, they participated in peace movements and anti-war demonstrations to voice their strong feelings against war and destruction of any kind. They motorcycled around the farmlands of New Jersey and spent many hours outdoors with each other, enjoying their deep love and appreciation of nature. They daydreamed of how life should be.

Susan and Stephen were married in 1969 and moved to Colorado to begin life together in the mountains, where Susan did freelance writing at home and Stephen researched solar energy in a laboratory. On the weekends, they began experimenting with printing Susan's poems, surrounded by Stephen's art, on posters that they silk-screened in their basement. They loved being together so much that it did not take long for them to begin disliking the 9-to-5 weekday separation that had resulted from their pursuing different careers. They soon decided that their being together, not just on weekends but all of the time, was more important than anything else, so Stephen left his research position in the laboratory. They packed their pick-up-truck camper with the silk-screened posters they had made, and they began a year of traveling together in the camper and selling their posters in towns and cities across the country. Their love of life and for one another, which they so warmly communicate, touched the public. People wanted more of

Susan's deep, rich thoughts on life, love, family, friendship, and nature presented in the emotion-stirring colors and rhythmic drawings of Stephen's highly sensitive art. And so, in 1972, in response to incredible public demand, their first book, COME INTO THE MOUNTAINS, DEAR FRIEND, was published, and history was made in the process. Today, after seventeen years of marriage and spending all of their time together, Susan and Stephen continue to share their love with all of us.

In addition to this book, Susan has authored eight best-selling books of poetry: COME INTO THE MOUNTAINS, DEAR FRIEND; I WANT TO LAUGH, I WANT TO CRY; PEACE FLOWS FROM THE SKY; SOMEONE ELSE TO LOVE; YOURS IF YOU ASK; LOVE, LIVE AND SHARE; FIND HAPPINESS IN EVERYTHING YOU DO; and DON'T BE AFRAID TO LOVE. Susan's poems have been published on over 200 million greeting cards and have appeared in numerous national and international magazines and high school and college textbooks. She has edited books by other well-known authors and has coauthored a woman's health book entitled TAKE CHARGE OF YOUR BODY. Susan continues to work on her autobiography and also writes music. She is currently recording her poems on cassettes to the accompaniment of contemplative background music.

In addition to designing and illustrating all of Susan's books, Stephen's art complements the words of many other well-known authors. He creates beautiful greeting cards and calendars, which feature his special airbrush and watercolor blends, his beautiful oil paintings, and his unique calligraphy. Stephen is an accomplished photographer and continues to study physics as a hobby. Together, he and Susan participate in many outdoor sports, such as hiking in the mountains, swimming in the ocean, and cross-country skiing along the Continental Divide.

Susan and Stephen have three children. They spend all of their time with their family, including their children in everything that they do. Half of their time is spent traveling, and the other half is spent working together in their studio in Colorado. Theirs is an atmosphere of joy, love, and spontaneous creativity as they continue to produce the words, the poems, the rhythm, and the art that has reached around the world, opening the hearts and enriching the lives of more than 500 million people in every country, in every language, in every culture. Truly, our world is a happier place because of this perfectly matched and beautifully blended couple, Susan Polis Schutz and Stephen Schutz.

Photo by Jared

Susan Polis Schutz

Stephen Schutz

Jordanna

*The threat of a nuclear holocaust was created by human beings and therefore human beings can and must "uncreate" that threat. **Mothers Embracing Nuclear Disarmament (MEND)** is a non-profit educational group working to inspire all men and women to embrace peace for the sake of future generations. You can help.*
*Write **MEND National Office**, P.O. Box 2309A, La Jolla, CA 92038.*